Active Every Day,
LOWER kS2

Active Every Day
LOWER KS2

10-minute activities
for a healthy school day

Linda Kelly • Wendy Seward

A & C Black • London

Published in 2006 by A & C Black Publishers Ltd
38 Soho Square, London W1D 3HB
www.acblack.com

ISBN-10: 0 7136 7728 7
ISBN-13: 978 0 7136 7728 7

Note: While every effort has been made to ensure that the content of this
book is as technically accurate and as sound as possible, neither the author nor
the publisher can accept responsibility for any injury or loss sustained as a result
of the use of this material.

A & C Black uses paper produced with elemental chlorine-free pulp,
harvested from managed sustainable forests.

Acknowledgements
Cover illustration by Sheilagh Noble
Textual illustrations by Celia Hart
Cover and inside design by Fiona Grant

Typeset by Palimpsest Book Production Ltd, Grangemouth, Stirlingshire
Printed and bound in Great Britain by Caligraving Ltd, Thetford

Contents

Introduction

Why is physical activity important?

The importance of physical activity, and its links to improved levels of attainment, is nothing new. In fact, the notion of 'a healthy mind and a healthy body' is firmly embedded in history. The emphasis placed by the Government on the value of exercise and its links to the health and welfare of the nation are well documented, not only in terms of the obvious physical benefits but also in relation to citizenship and Personal, Health and Social Education (PHSE). Indeed, there are many benefits to be gained by children engaging in regular physical activity. These include:

- essential health benefits – developing an efficient, healthy heart and building strong muscles and bones;

- the reduction of body fat – exercise coupled with a sensible diet can vastly reduce the rate of obesity, which is rising in the UK;

- mental health benefits – physical activity can reduce stress and anxiety;

- the development of a healthy lifestyle;

- continued involvement in physical activity and sport;

- making children feel good about themselves;

- the improvement of children's social skills;

- enhanced concentration and focus.

The National Healthy Schools Programme views regular physical activity for all pupils as an essential component of becoming a healthy school. The first of their aims is that the National Healthy Schools Programme will 'support children and young people in developing healthy behaviours'. It then explains that in order to become a healthy school certain procedures must be put into place, so that 'pupils are provided with a range of opportunities to be physically active. They understand how physical activity can help them to be more healthy, and how physical activity can improve and be part of their everyday life'.

The Government's vision for children's services, 'Every Child Matters', has five key outcomes. Two of these are 'Be Healthy' and 'Enjoy and Achieve'; like the National Healthy

Schools Programme, this provides a vision of all young people being involved in regular physical activity, having a healthy lifestyle, achieving personal and social development and enjoying recreation.

Therefore, daily physical activity should, and could quite easily, be built into every school day and every child's learning.

Why every day?

It would be difficult to think of anyone who would not agree that regular exercise is important, but why should children take part in physical activity *every day*?

- Exercise is habit forming, so needs to be undertaken regularly.

- Regular repetition of an activity leads to improvement.

- Health benefits will be observed if exercise is undertaken every day.

- To stimulate mind and body.

- To provide a balance between activity and inactivity during the day.

Recommended levels of activity

The long-term ambition of the Department for Education & Skills (DfES) and the Department for Culture, Media & Sport (DCMS) is that by 2010 children will be able to participate in at least four hours of sport each week. This will be made up of:

- at least two hours of high-quality PE and sport at school, with the expectation that this will be delivered totally within the curriculum;

- an additional 2–3 hours beyond the school day, delivered by a range of school, community and club providers (DfES and DCMS, 2003).

The government hopes that 85 per cent of all pupils aged between 5 and 16 will have achieved the minimum of two hours of high-quality PE and school sport in and out of the curriculum by 2008. The Review Group on Physical Education in Scotland (2004) also states that 'all schools and education authorities should be working towards meeting the recommendations of the Physical Activity Strategy and the Sport 21 Strategy of providing two hours' quality physical education for each child every week'. It is anticipated that this would be the minimum provision that schools would offer, since it is less than the time recommended by the British Heart Foundation, who state that for improved health 'children and young people should aim to participate in activity of at least moderate intensity for one hour every day'. The Department of Health document *Choosing Health? Choosing Activity* (2004) also concurs that 'children and young people should achieve a total of at least 60 minutes of at least moderate physical activity each day'.

This can be seen as a reaction to the rising levels of obesity in the young. According to *Choosing Health? Choosing Activity*, 16 per cent of 2–15-year-olds are now obese, which brings increased risk of health problems such as hypertension, heart disease and type 2 diabetes. The study states that we need an education system that promotes and enables physical activity. This means ensuring that children are taught in active play and that PE and activity are an integral part of every day.

Choosing Health? Choosing Activity also recommends that activity sessions in schools can be achieved very satisfactorily through several short bouts of activity of 10 minutes or more, which is the philosophy behind *Active Every Day*. We are not suggesting that *Active Every Day* should replace the two hours of physical education to which all pupils are entitled; rather, it should be seen as additional and used during the day where it will be of most benefit.

Why do the *Active Every Day* programme?

Only a few schools have developed a dedicated programme of daily physical activity, despite the fact that research has shown that the brain requires certain conditions to be able to operate to its optimum capacity (Scheuer and Mitchell, 2003). These conditions include a good supply of oxygen and the release of certain chemicals – two things that happen when we take part in physical exercise. So, a small investment of 10 minutes a day of physical activity can pay huge dividends in the classroom, with children being more focused and more willing to learn. In the long term, this could potentially play an instrumental part in improving levels of attainment and enabling each child to reach his or her full potential.

Also, if children are given a positive experience of physical activity at school, this will lay the foundations for a lifetime's involvement in regular exercise. Routines established at a young age tend to be ingrained for life, so a firm commitment to 10-minute bursts of activity, as and when required, coupled with an effective and progressive PE curriculum, should go some way to instilling in children the routine and advantages of daily activity. What better habit to develop than an improved understanding of how the body works and an enhanced opportunity to develop a healthy lifestyle?

It is clear from the research carried out into the links between physical activity and health, and the high profile that physical activity now demands on the political agenda, that this is a very real issue requiring immediate attention. *Active Every Day* does not claim to provide a 'magic bullet' that will cure all of society's ills; however, it does go some way towards improving and increasing the time given to exercise and its undeniable benefits to the nation's young people.

How to use the programme

The *Active Every Day* programme is a collection of 10-minute activities that teachers can fit in at any time during the school day, wherever and whenever it is felt to be convenient or necessary. The activities can also be formally timetabled if preferred; however, experience has found that they are better suited to being used as a response to children's (and teachers') immediate needs and should therefore be dictated by those who will most benefit from them. For example, children might have just undertaken a particularly difficult numeracy lesson and need 10 minutes of physical activity to recharge their batteries and energise their brains ready for the next lesson, and a particularly tricky concept may become less daunting if it is preceded by a short burst of adrenaline before embarking on the independent element of the task.

Some of the activities have been specially designed to be carried out in the classroom with the minimum of equipment or disruption; these would be ideal precursors to independent or group activities. Others need a larger space such as a hall or playground and may need a small amount of equipment, although the preparation time required is negligible – an important concern in a teacher's already stretched timetable! Many of the activities have ideas for extension and simplification to suit the children with whom you are working. However, as with any resource, they may need to be adapted further to suit individuals within your class.

Music could be added to activities if desired. This could be used to change the possible pace of the session, making it more active or slowing down at the end of the activity.

All of the activities are devised to be fun, enjoyable and inclusive, as well as having the obvious physical and social benefits that accompany interactive physical participation. Children who enjoy an activity are more likely to remember it, and will often replicate it with friends in the playground or outside of school, thus increasing the potential for activity as opposed to inactivity. It should not be forgotten that fun and enjoyment are integral to children's learning and development.

The programme is divided into six main sections for ease of use and can be delivered in any order and at any time. There is also an additional section concentrating on warm-ups, cool-downs, stretching and mobility. This section includes a selection of stretching and mobilising activities that can be performed in addition to the main activity. It also contains some simple ideas for warming up and cooling down, focusing on the important principles of both. There is also an appendix, which includes some photocopiable material that can be used by the teacher if desired. These include:

- a daily physical activity record sheet for pupils, which could be used at the start and end of each term or year to show progression;

- a weekly physical activity diary for pupils, which could be used at any time to examine patterns or amounts of activity;

- a physical activity attitude questionnaire for pupils, to inform the teacher's planning;

- an activity checklist for the teacher to keep a record of which activities have been undertaken and which ones were successful.

Each of the six sections gives teachers a range of age-related ideas that they can undertake with their class. The sections are as follows:

1. Limited space activities

These activities can be performed quite easily in the classroom with a minimum of disruption. Many of them require little or no movement of furniture – only that children stand in a space behind their desks – and most require no resources. The focus is on improving children's ability to listen carefully to instructions and complete a particular task or set of tasks.

2. Control, coordination and accuracy

These activities focus on the use of basic body control, coordination and accuracy in order to perform a selection of tasks, using a variety of basic sporting equipment including balls, rackets, beanbags and targets – all equipment that should be readily available in most schools.

3. Teamwork and cooperation

These activities involve the children working as a team or a group to complete a task. Participants are required to unite as a group and show consideration for the rest of the team. This section complements much of the work being done in the PHSE curriculum and can be easily linked to circle times.

4. Stamina, speed and agility

This group of activities gives pupils the chance to experience how their breathing changes with different types of exercise. It also examines the differences between speed and stamina and looks to increase agility and awareness. These activities represent an ideal opportunity for cross-curricular links to the science and physical education programmes of study.

5. Action rhymes

This collection of traditional action rhymes is excellent for developing coordination and improving children's ability to follow a sequence of instructions. They can be adapted to suit the individual or group of children as required. Older children can even be called upon to draft and perform rhymes of their own – they often find 'rap' style poetry good fun, and the rhymes can be linked to a literacy lesson.

6. Skipping activities

These activities involve limited equipment, but can have a huge impact on children's development and coordination. A range of schools across the country have publicly advocated the benefits of skipping and have rolled out the idea to include promoting positive play in the playground, even developing skipping clubs and demonstration teams. An element of care should be taken with skipping exercises as they can be strenuous and are deemed to be relatively high-impact activities. Rest time should always be built into the 10 minutes allocated.

Timetabling issues

The advantage of the *Active Every Day* programme is its simplicity and flexibility. It can be implemented very easily in to the school timetable: there is no prescribed time in the day when the 10 minutes of activity should be carried out, so the teacher can use his or her discretion to implement a session when his or her class would benefit the most. The ideas in the programme require no additional resources other than those usually found in a primary school, therefore demanding no additional budgetary requirements. The activities can be undertaken in a variety of settings including the classroom, school hall, corridor or playground.

There is usually little point in introducing a session immediately before break or lunchtime, or immediately after. However, a wet day, when the children have been restricted to the school building over lunchtime, could prove an ideal time to focus on a controlled burst of activity to reactivate the brain ready for learning to take place.

The idea behind *Active Every Day* is to re-energise the children so they will be ready to focus on the next part of their learning. As a result, it is important that the children are allowed to cool down to an acceptable level to continue with their education. It is important that the teacher selects an appropriate activity to achieve this.
Active Every Day could easily be used to complement a school's existing system of rewards; however, withdrawal of the 10 minutes is not recommended as a punishment as this would negate the whole philosophy of the belief that exercise is an intrinsic part of everyday life.

Developing a whole-school approach to physical activity

Schools are increasingly committed to creating a healthy school environment. One of the aims of this is to try to stem the worryingly high numbers of overweight and obese children. In order to achieve success in this area, there needs to be a whole-school approach to the promotion of physical activity and a commitment to healthy living. This is often highlighted in whole-school policies, particularly in relation to the 'Every Child Matters' agenda and the relevant links to the National Healthy Schools Standard.

To increase levels of physical activity, a school needs enthusiastically to promote and enable regular participation in a variety of key areas. These could include:

- a broad and balanced high-quality PE curriculum

- actively promoting 'Walk to School Weeks'

- walking buses

- active and positive play in the playground

- links to the School Sport Coordinator Programme

- 'wake and shake' clubs

- high-quality out of school hours learning (OSHL)

- sports days

- regular inter-school competitions

- regular intra-school competitions

- non-competitive sports festivals

- attractive notice boards giving clear messages

- regular rewards assemblies

- links to local clubs and other agencies

- participation in the *Active Every Day* programme.

Combined with the above, schools should actively promote a campaign of healthy eating and drinking. Consultation with school meal providers and the recent publicity surrounding Jamie Oliver's initiative have brought the issue of improving school meals firmly onto the political agenda. As a result, there has never been a better time to re-educate both parents and children as to the benefits and value of proper nutrition. Schools can actively promote healthy eating and drinking in the following ways:

- healthy snacks for breaktime

- fizzy drinks off the menu

- healthy food and drinks in vending machines

- 'design a healthy menu' competition

- water fountains around the school

- individual water bottles for each pupil

- pupils allowed to drink water as they need it

- parental workshops and discussion groups.

Safety considerations

Each activity in this manual includes appropriate safety tips, but there are also some general issues that teachers must be aware of when undertaking physical activity.

Limited space activities
If activities are to be performed in the classroom, makes sure that the children have sufficient room to swing their arms or legs without injuring themselves or others. Check that there is nothing on the floor that could be tripped over or anything protruding that could be bumped into.

Hall activities

Ensure that the floor is free from debris including food, mud or litter. Keep the activity away from free-standing equipment such as pianos or music stands.

Outside/playground activities

Check the surface to be used to ensure that there is no broken glass, loose gravel or anything children could slip on and hurt themselves. Ensure that any activity you are doing is well away from any boundary walls or fences. Some of the activities involve children running at quite high speeds; these should be avoided if the area is wet or slippery.

Clothing and footwear

Children do not have to change in to PE kit for these activities as this would eat in to the allocated 10 minutes, but correct footwear must be worn. Pupils should wear training shoes for outside work and trainers/pumps or bare feet for the activities in the hall or classroom, depending on the nature of the activity.

Jewellery

Children should not wear jewellery while performing the activities as it can injure both themselves and other children.

Water

Children should have access to drinking water and be allowed to drink when necessary. During a 10-minute activity session it is unlikely that children will need to drink, but at the conclusion of the session water should be freely available.

Not immediately after eating

It would not be sensible to use the *Active Every Day* programme directly after eating lunch as there is plenty of running and jumping included. Since the programme should ideally be used as a response to the needs of children and a break from their structured timetable, a session at this time is unlikely to be warranted.

High-impact activities

Care must be taken with some of the 'Skipping' and 'Stamina, speed and agility' activities as they can be strenuous and potentially dangerous for young children's growing bones, muscles and joints. Some might be considered to be relatively high-impact activities, so rest time should always be built into the allocated 10 minutes.

Warming up, Cooling down, mobilising and stretching

One of the major benefits of the *Active Every Day* programme is that the children do not need to perform a traditional warm-up, as most of the activities are in fact warm-ups in themselves. However, if you feel the need to add in a warm-up or cool-down activity as well as some mobilising and stretching activities, here are some suggestions and general principles.

Warming up

A warm-up should always start slowly and build up speed gradually. The teacher can lead this activity with the children starting off standing on the spot. The children can then begin by moving various parts of their bodies, including the fingers, toes, legs and arms. The head and trunk can also be included. Children can then include actions that move them from the spot, for example walking, jogging, skipping and so on.

Cooling down

A cool-down at the end of an activity session allows children to slow down and recover, ensuring they are ready to return to their normal class. Activities can be the reverse of the warm-up, culminating in the children performing slow movements in a stationary position.

Active Every Day: Lower Key Stage 2 © Linda Kelly and Wendy Seward 2006, A & C Black Publishers Ltd

Mobilising joints

These exercises help to loosen the joints and make them ready for exercise. They need to be performed slowly and with control. Children can perform 5–10 of each exercise, but must ensure they repeat the exercise on each side of the body (that is with both legs/arms).

Waist twists

Purpose
To loosen and warm up your waist and middle.

How to perform
Face the front with your knees slightly bent. Keep your feet facing the front and twist the top half of your body around to one side, then repeat on the opposite side. Your arms should be up level with your shoulders with your elbows bent and palms facing down.

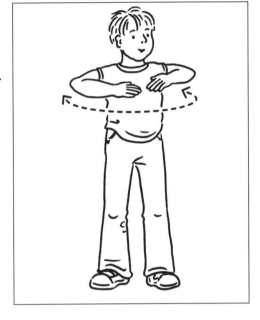

Side bends

Purpose
To loosen and warm up your lower back and sides.

How to perform
Stand straight with your feet shoulder-width apart and your hands on your hips. Bend to the side without tilting forwards or back. Your knees should be slightly bent at all times.

Shoulder rolls

Purpose
To loosen and warm up your shoulders.

How to perform
Make sure you are in a space. Keep your arms slightly bent and move them in a circular motion, both backwards and forwards. Make sure you move them in both directions on both sides of the body.

Knee-lifts

Purpose
To loosen and warm up your knee and hip joints.

How to perform
Stand facing the front. Lift one knee up, keeping the rest of your body upright. Perform a clap under your lifted knee. Repeat with the other knee.

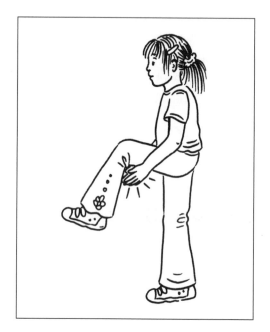

Static stretches

You can select three or four stretches appropriate to the activity and include them during a warm-up or as part of a cool-down. The stretches should be performed slowly and with control, and held for a count of 6–10 seconds. Remember to stretch both sides of the body. Make sure you breathe when stretching.

Whole-body stretch (standing)

Purpose
To stretch all your major muscles.

How to perform
Stand up straight, facing the front. Reach up tall with both hands, as far as possible. Keep your feet flat on the floor to avoid overbalancing.

Whole-body stretch (lying)

Purpose
To stretch all your major muscles.

How to perform
Lie down on your back (on a mat if possible). Stretch your arms above your head – they should be touching your ears – and point your toes.

Quads (front of upper leg) stretch

Purpose
To stretch the muscles in the front of your upper leg.

How to perform
Lie down on your front (on a mat if possible). Reach behind you and hold your ankle. Push your hip into the floor.

Groin stretch

Purpose
To stretch the muscles in your groin area.

How to perform
Sit on the floor with your head and upper body straight. Bend your knees and press your feet together. Push gently down on the inside of your legs with your elbows.

Hamstring (back of upper leg) stretch

Purpose
To stretch your hamstring (back of upper leg) muscles.

How to perform
Stand straight and put one leg out in front of you. Keep that leg straight and take your weight on to the back leg. Slightly bend the back/supporting leg. Tilt your bottom slightly forwards.

Calf (back of lower leg) stretch

Purpose
To stretch your calf (back of lower leg) muscles.

How to perform
Stand facing the front with both feet facing forwards. Keep your back leg straight with your heels on the floor. Bend your front leg and lean forwards slightly.

Chest stretch

Purpose
To stretch the muscles across your chest.

How to perform
Stand up straight. Put your hands at the base of your spine, facing downwards. Squeeze your elbows together.

Triceps (bottom of upper arm) stretch

Purpose
To stretch your triceps (bottom of upper arm) muscles.

How to perform
Stand facing the front. Take one hand and place it over your shoulder, reaching down to the centre of your back. Use your other hand to keep the elbow high.

Dynamic stretching

These dynamic stretching exercises are fantastic as they stretch and mobilise the muscles and joints in one exercise. They should be performed steadily and with control.

Walking high knee-lift

Purpose
To work on buttock flexibility and hip and shoulder mobility.

How to perform
Walk slowly forwards, bringing your knee up to create right angles at your knee and hips. At the same time, bring up the opposite arm to create right angles at the elbow and shoulder.

Walking lunges

Purpose
To stretch the front of the hip and thigh.

How to perform
Walk slowly and, as you step forwards, bend your knees so your back knee touches the floor. Your back heel will come off the floor. Ensure that you keep the top half of your body upright.

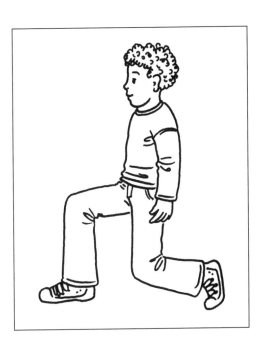

Active Every Day: Lower Key Stage 2 © Linda Kelly and Wendy Seward 2006, A & C Black Publishers Ltd

Heel flicks

Purpose
To stretch the front and back of your thighs.

How to perform
Jog forwards, flicking your heels up to touch your bottom. Put your hands behind your back on your bottom with the palms facing out. To be done correctly, each flick must touch your hands.

Walking hamstring stretches

Purpose
To stretch your hamstring (back of the thigh) muscles.

How to perform
Walk slowly to a count of four and, on every fourth step, straighten your front leg and sink down on to your back leg. This leg should bend, and you can push down on to it with your hands. The toes of your front leg should be pointing up.

Walking single knee-lifts

Purpose
To work on buttock flexibility and hip mobility.

How to perform
Walk slowly to a count of three, bringing your knee up to create a right angle at your knee and hip on every third step. After doing 10 lifts to one leg, repeat on the other leg.

One, Two, Three

- Ask the children to stand to the side of their desk or table facing a partner. Give each child a letter – either A or B.

- A starts by saying 'one', B follows this with 'two' and A then counts 'three'. B starts again with 'one', A with 'two' and B with 'three'.

- Continue until the children are comfortable with the three-number pattern.

- Now, ask the children to replace 'one' with a clap, so instead of saying 'one' the children clap their hands. 'Two' and 'three' are spoken as before.

- Once the children are comfortable with this, tell them to replace 'two' with a stomp on the floor. So, the pattern is now 'clap', 'stomp', 'three'.

- Next, tell the children to replace 'three' with a nod. So, instead of 'one', 'two, 'three' the pattern is now 'clap', 'stomp', 'nod'.

Suggested space Classroom

Learning outcomes To work cooperatively with a partner; to learn and remember a movement pattern.

Resources None

Health and safety Ensure that the children are well spaced out and away from their desks so they can clap and stomp safely.

Simplification Instead of working with a partner, divide the class in to two teams, A and B. Each group calls out the pattern together to help each other.

Extension Tell the children to select their own actions to replace 'one, two and three'. Ask the children to perform their action sequence to the rest of the class.

Limited space

Sporting Heroes

- This activity is based on the popular game of 'Simon Says'

- Ask the children to start marching on the spot.

- Tell them that you will call out the name of a sporting hero and they have to strike a pose based on the named hero's sport. So, if you call out 'David Beckham' they have to strike a football pose (for example, kicking a ball) and if you call out 'Ben Cohen' they have to strike a rugby pose (for example running with the ball).

- After striking the pose, the children should start marching on the spot again until you name another hero and they strike another pose.

- After several poses, explain that they can only strike a pose if the sporting hero's name is accompanied by your name, for example 'Mrs Jones says: David Beckham' (relate to 'Simon Says'). If anyone strikes a pose without your name being given first, that child loses a life. Tell the children that they each start with three lives and when they've all been lost they are out.

- The last child left becomes the leader for the next game.

Suggested space Classroom or corridor

Learning outcomes To listen carefully to instructions and carry them out; to create a simple action pose.

Resources None

Health and safety Ensure that there is enough room for the children to strike the poses.

Simplification Call out the name of the activity rather than the name of the sports star.

Extension Ask the children to research sporting heroes to introduce to the game.

Mirror Image

- Ask the children to get into pairs, facing their partner. Number them 1 and 2.

- Ask number 1 to perform a movement on the spot, for example waving his/her hands above his/her head. Tell number 2 to observe and copy the movement, as if they were a mirror image.

- Ask number 1 to choose a second movement, for example turning around on the spot, and tell number 2 to copy the movement.

- Next, tell number 1 to repeat the first and second movements for number 2 to observe and copy.

- Tell the children to continue, either using single movements or starting to develop a sequence, depending upon the ability of the class or individual children.

- After about a minute, change the lead child so number 2 begins.

- Ask the children, 'Which movements are easier to copy?' and 'How do you remember which movement comes next?'

Suggested space A clear space in the classroom or the hall

Learning outcomes To be able to devise and copy a short exercise, revising and improving initial ideas; to work cooperatively with a partner.

Resources None

Health and safety Make sure there is plenty of room for swinging arms and legs.

Simplification Tell child number 2 to copy and repeat the movement rather than mirror it.

Extension Include a sequence using different body parts, for example one hand movement, one leg movement, one head movement, one movement of the trunk and one high and one low movement.

Limited space

Count the Seconds

- Ask the children to stand either behind their desks or in a space in the area that is being used, all facing the same way.

- Start the stopwatch and tell the children when 30 seconds have passed.

- Repeat the process, but this time tell the children to sit down quietly when they think 30 seconds have passed.

- Watch the class to see how accurate the children are at judging the allocated time.

- Talk to the children about counting for themselves and making up their own minds instead of sitting down when others do.

- You can repeat the activity with the children keeping their eyes closed so their decision about when to sit down is not influenced by the rest of the class.

Suggested space Classroom, hall, corridor or outside space

Learning outcomes To be able to count up to 30; to work independently and make your own decisions.

Resources A stopwatch

Health and safety Ensure the children open their eyes before they sit down.

Simplification Ask the children to judge shorter timescales, for example only 10 or 20 seconds.

Extension Ask the children to judge longer timescales, for example one minute.

At the Sports Centre I ...

- Ask the children to stand behind their chairs in their table groups.

- Ask the first child in the group to begin by saying 'At the Sports Centre I . . .' and adding the name of a sport, then performing an action to illustrate that sport. For example, the child could say 'At the Sports Centre I played tennis' and pretend to hit a ball with a tennis racket. All the children in the group should copy the action.

- The second child then repeats the first sport and then adds another, for example 'At the Sports Centre I played tennis and went swimming', and does the tennis action and then pretends to be swimming. Again, all the children in the group should copy the actions.

- The third child repeats the first two sports and then adds another, for example 'At the Sports Centre I played tennis, went swimming and ran 100 metres' and again performs the actions. As before, as each person speaks all the children in the group perform the actions.

- The target is to list as many different sports as possible before some are forgotten. If a child forgets one of the sports, tell their group to start again and try to beat their best score.

- You can discuss strategies for remembering the order of activities. For example, 'Is it possible to use the alphabet to help you remember the order?'

Suggested space Classroom

Learning outcomes To copy and extend a sequence; to take turns cooperatively.

Resources None

Health and safety Make sure there is enough room to carry out the activity safely and effectively.

Simplification Put the children in to mixed ability groups.

Extension Ask the children to repeat the list in reverse order. Introduce a time element, for example 'How many activities can your team remember in two minutes?'

Limited space

Mix 'n' Match

- Ask the pupils to walk steadily around the area, taking care to avoid each other and the furniture.

- Tell them that when you say 'change' they have to change direction and continue walking steadily around the area. Repeat this several times.

- Next, roll both dice and call out the body parts highlighted, for example 'hands and knees'.

- The children now turn to the nearest person and join the two body parts, for example hands to hands and knees to knees or hand to knee and hand to knee.

- Stop and discuss possible combinations with the children.

- Repeat the activity several times.

Suggested space Classroom or corridor

Learning outcomes To name different parts of the body; to work cooperatively and sensibly with a number of different children.

Resources Two large dice, both clearly showing a different body part on each face, for example hands, toes, hips, elbows, knees and shoulders.

Health and safety Discuss with the children the need to look up and ahead to avoid obstacles.

Simplification Use only one die.

Extension Ask the children to work in groups of four. Use more extensive names for the parts of the body to extend vocabulary.

Last Letter First

- Ask the children to find a partner and stand facing each other in a space by their desk.

- Tell the first child to say a word, for example 'dog'. They can say any noun.

- The next child then has to say a word that begins with the last letter of the previous word, for example 'gate'.

- The first child then says a word that begins with the last letter of that word, for example 'egg'.

- When the children are able to do this, ask them to add claps after they have said their word. The number of claps should be the same as the number of letters in the word, so 'dog' equals three claps.

- Tell the children that the next child has to be ready with his/her word as soon as the claps have finished.

Suggested space Classroom

Learning outcomes To work on mental agility and spelling; to perform simple actions in response to a given task.

Resources None

Health and safety Make sure the children stand up straight and look their partner in the eye.

Simplification All words to be only three letters long.

Extension Words can be longer and there can be penalties for children who aren't ready with the next word.

Limited space

Don't Break the Chain!

- Ask the children to form a rough circle around the outside of the classroom, making sure they can see the person on either side of them.

- Start the activity by putting your right arm straight out in front of you with the palm facing down, and tell the child to your left to copy you, then the child to their left and so on.

- When everyone in the circle has their right arm out, start the next action by putting your left arm straight out in front of you with the palm down. Again, all the children in the circle should copy you, one by one.

- Next, introduce more actions such as a clap, a turn on the spot or turning your arms so the palms are facing up.

- Emphasise the need for teamwork and concentration so the chain is not broken and the action runs smoothly around the circle.

Suggested space Classroom

Learning outcomes To work cooperatively as a class to achieve an outcome; to use simple movement patterns to achieve a required outcome.

Resources None

Health and safety Make sure that the children can see the person next to them clearly.

Simplification Children can perform the activity in small groups of 4–6.

Extension Use more complex actions and increase the speed.

Create a Character

Arrange the children into mixed ability pairs and give the children a number – either 1 or 2.

Ask the number 1s to arrange their partners into a particular type of sporting character – for example move their arms, legs and head to create an Olympic sprinter or a champion golfer – without telling their partner what type of sporting character they are making them into.

After a minute or two, call 'freeze frame', which means that the number 2s have to hold their position.

Next, give the number 2s three chances to guess their sporting character, for example 'Am I a sprinter?' and so on.

If they get it right first time they get three points, if they get it right second time they get two points and if they get it right third time they get one point.

If they don't guess it after three goes, their partner wins the point. They can then swap roles and start again.

Ask the children, 'How can you make someone look like they are running?' and 'Is it different for a sprint and a jog?'

Suggested space Classroom

Learning outcomes To identify the differences between the actions needed for a sprint and a jog; to work creatively and cooperatively with a partner.

Resources None

Health and safety Take care when moving your partner – be aware of the limitations of movement.

Simplification The children can work on their own and you tell them which sport to imitate.

Extension Two pairs can join together and create a double position, for example two tennis players.

Limited space

Squeeze Me

- Ask the children to hold hands and form a large circle around the outside of the classroom. You should be in the circle as well.

- Start the activity by squeezing the hand of the child to your right.

- When he/she feels the squeeze, he/she then squeezes the hand of the next child in the circle. In this way, the squeeze is passed around the circle until it is back with you.

- Do the same thing again, but this time going to the left.

- Discuss strategies with the children. Ask them, 'How quickly can we get around the circle?' and 'Can we beat our time?'

Suggested space Classroom

Learning outcomes To work cooperatively as a whole class; to improve levels of coordination and awareness.

Resources None

Health and safety Make sure your hands are clean before you take part in this activity. Discuss cleanliness (links to PHSE).

Simplification Children can work in small groups of about 6–8.

Extension Children can repeat the exercise with their eyes shut.

Pass and Repeat

- Divide the class into groups of approximately eight children with one ball per group.

- Split each group into two smaller groups (so two groups of four) and ask each group to form a line. The two lines should be facing each other, about five metres apart.

- Give a ball to the child at the front of one of the lines. On your signal, he or she passes to the child at the head of the opposite line, then runs to the back of that line (so they are running in the direction of the ball). The objective is for the receiving child to catch the ball cleanly.

- The child who caught the ball should now throw it to the next child in the opposite line and run to the back of that line, and the activity continues in this way.

- Tell the children to use a chest pass to throw the ball.

- If any of the children drop the ball, stop the activity and remind them that the aim is to catch the ball cleanly, then restart the game.

Suggested space Hall or outside space

Learning outcomes To throw and catch with accuracy; to improve levels of fitness.

Resources One ball per group

Health and safety Tell the children to keep their eyes on the ball at all times and be ready to catch it when they are at the front of the line.

Simplification Reduce the speed of the activity and use a larger, softer ball.

Extension Increase the speed of the activity.

Control, coordination and accuracy

Don't Let it Fall!

- Give each child a tennis racket and a tennis ball and ask them to find a space in the playground where they are able to move around.

- First, tell the children to try to hold the tennis ball on the racket without it rolling off.

- Next, ask them to move around slowly, still without losing their tennis ball.

- Now, ask them to try to keep the tennis ball moving up and down while standing still, then to try to keep the tennis ball moving up and down while moving around.

- Finally, challenge the class to keep their tennis balls moving up and down while following a lead child (alternatively, you could lead the group). If any child loses his or her ball, that child is out.

- As the number of children left in the game reduces, you could increase the speed of the movement to a jog or a 'bounce up – bounce down'.

- You could give the last remaining pupil a school reward such as a house point, if your school has such a system.

- Ask the children, 'How did you keep the ball close to your racket?' and 'How did you avoid bumping into other children?'

Suggested space Playground

Learning outcomes To work on basic racket and ball skills; to use the space cooperatively.

Resources One tennis racket/plastic bat and one tennis ball/sponge ball per child

Health and safety Be aware of the other children moving around you at all times.

Simplification Use a bean bag instead of a tennis ball.

Extension Make the activity more challenging by introducing obstacles such as cones for the children to move around.

Olympic Games

- Set the chairs out in a circle, with one chair in the middle.

- Ask the children to sit in one of the chairs around the edge of the circle.

- Give each of the children the name of an Olympic sport, for example long jump, high jump, discus, javelin, shot put and so on, going round the circle in order. There should be about five of each sport in an average class.

- Sit down in the chair in the middle of the circle and call out the name of one of the sports.

- You and all of the children who have been given that sport have to get up and try to sit down in one of the empty chairs around the edge of the circle. Moving to the chair to either side of you is not allowed.

- The child who is left standing has to take the centre seat and be the caller for the next round, and the game continues in this way.

- At any point the caller can say 'Olympic Games', which means that everybody has to get up and move to a different chair.

Suggested space Clear space in a classroom or the hall

Learning outcomes To listen carefully to instructions and to act upon them; to work on body control in a confined space.

Resources One chair for each child.

Health and safety Regularly remind the children not to push to get to a chair.

Extension Pupils cannot return to a chair if they have been there before.

Control, coordination and accuracy

Catch and Release

- Ask the children to get into pairs and give each pair a tennis ball.

- Tell them to stand one to two metres apart and start throwing the ball to each other.

- After 10 successful throws and catches they can take a step back so that they are slightly further apart.

- After 10 more successful throws and catches they can take another step back.

- If either of them drops the ball, they have to take a step closer to each other.

- Ask the children, 'How could you make the throw or catch more successful?' Tie the question in to any specific problems each pair is having.

Suggested space Hall or outside space

Learning outcomes To improve hand–eye coordination.

Resources One tennis ball per pair (two per pair for the extension).

Health and safety Always keep your eye on the ball to maximise the chance of catching it.

Simplification Use a larger ball.

Extension Use two tennis balls per pair. As one pupil releases one ball, the other pupil releases the other one.

Mini Olympics

● Ask the children to find a space where they have enough room to swing their arms.

● Call out a sport that is taking place at the Olympics. The children respond by performing the appropriate action (you can demonstrate these at the beginning of the activity):

  ● Running — Jog around the area, avoiding the other children

  ● Jumping — Jump on the spot

  ● Tennis match — In pairs, mime hitting the ball to each other

  ● Cycling race — Lie on your back and do cycling actions with your legs

  ● Basketball match — Mime dribbling and shooting the ball

  ● Rowing race — Find a partner and stand one in front of the other, then move slowly backwards doing rowing actions

● Ask the children, 'What did you do to make sure you didn't bump into the other children?' and 'How did you remember what each action was?'

Suggested space Hall or dry outside space

Learning outcomes To remember and perform set commands and the appropriate accompanying actions; to work cooperatively in the space allowed; to improve levels of fitness and awareness.

Resources None

Health and safety Make sure the children are aware of each other, especially when moving backwards.

Simplification Start off by using only three of the commands.

Extension Change the instructions fairly quickly. Tell the children they can only use specific body parts to demonstrate the event, for example 'arms only' or 'legs only'.

Control, coordination and accuracy

15

Quick Release

- Ask the children to get themselves into groups of four.

- Give one member of each group a ball. This child should stand facing the other three children, two to three metres away from them.

- On your signal, the child with the ball passes to the first person in the line, who returns it. The thrower then passes to the next child in line, who again returns it. Continue until all three children have caught and returned the ball. The thrower then reverses the order back up the line.

- After one minute, tell the children to swap positions.

- Ask the children to count how many catches they make in the time allowed.

Suggested space Hall or playground

Learning outcomes To work on throwing, catching and speed of reactions.

Resources A large ball (for example, a size 4 netball or similar) for each group of four children. A stopwatch.

Health and safety Ensure that all the children are looking at the thrower when he or she has the ball.

Simplification Use a larger ball or move the children closer together.

Extension Use a stopwatch to time the groups and see which one is fastest.

16

Agility Ball

- Ask the children to get into pairs and stand back to back with one child holding the ball.

- Keeping his/her arms out straight, the child with the ball twists at the waist to pass the ball to the other child, who then twists to pass the ball back. Continue until they've passed the ball 10 times in one direction and 10 in the opposite direction.

- Next, the child with the ball reaches up and passes it overhead to his/her partner, who passes it back through their legs. This continues for 10 goes, then the partners change over so they each perform both actions.

- Finally, ask the partners to sit facing each other with their legs out straight and their toes touching. They have to roll the ball around their bodies, keeping it as close as possible, and repeat this five times.

- Ask the children, 'How did you make sure you didn't drop the ball or lose control?'

Suggested space Hall or outside space

Learning outcomes To work on ball control and flexibility; to work cooperatively with a partner.

Resources One size 4 ball per pair

Health and safety Ensure there is enough space between the children when they pass the ball overhead, as they will lean back slightly.

Simplification Use a larger ball.

Extension Use one hand only to do the ball rolling. Time each activity to see which pair is the quickest.

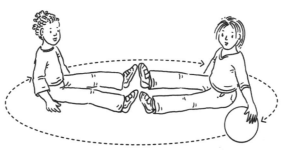

Bucket Bonanza

- Ask the children to get into groups of about six. Half of the group stand about two metres away from a bucket (or hoop), and the other half stand on the other side of the bucket, again about two metres away.

- When you blow a whistle or call 'throw', the first child in each group tries to throw their bean bag into the bucket.

- If they are successful, they run to the back of the opposite line and sit down.

- If they miss the bucket, they retrieve their bean bag and join the end of the line of the group opposite, ready to throw again.

- The children continue to throw until all of the bean bags have landed in the bucket or until you call time.

- The winning team is the first one with all of its players sitting down and all of their bean bags in the bucket.

- Ask the children, 'Why are some throws more successful than others?' and 'How can you improve your level of accuracy?'

- You can repeat the game with the children nearer or further away from the bucket, depending on the success of each group.

Suggested space Hall or playground

Learning outcomes To practise throwing at a target, adjusting and adapting previous attempts to improve upon performance.

Resources One bucket or hoop per group. One bean bag per person. Markers to indicate throwing line.

Health and safety Be aware of other people around you when you are running or throwing.

Simplification Reduce the distance of the throwers from the bucket.

Extension Increase the distance of the throwers from the bucket.

Active Every Day: Lower Key Stage 2 © Linda Kelly and Wendy Seward 2006, A & C Black Publishers Ltd

Catchers and Dodgers

- Ask the children to get into groups of about six and give each group a sequencing spot. Use the cones to mark out a playing area for each group (about one-third of a netball court).

- Four members of the group are the 'dodgers'. They place their sequencing spot somewhere in the playing area and start off with one foot touching the sequencing spot.

- The other two children are the 'catchers' and start off outside the playing area.

- On your signal the dodgers can start to move around the area and the catchers can enter the area and try to tag one of the dodgers.

- If they catch anyone, that child has to return to the sequencing spot and stand with one foot touching it until a fellow dodger tags them to release them.

- When all of the dodgers have been caught, new catchers are selected and the game begins again.

- You can change the 'catchers' and the 'dodgers' at any time by a pre-agreed signal.

Suggested space Hall or playground

Learning outcomes To use space wisely; to move and control the body in a small space.

Resources One sequencing spot per group of six. Four cones per group of six.

Health and safety Ensure the ground is dry to prevent accidents when moving and turning sharply.

Simplification Reduce the size of the playing area. Once children have been caught, they are out of the game.

Extension Increase the size of the playing area and the number of children per group.

Control, coordination and accuracy

Send and Receive

- Ask the children to get into groups of four and number them 1, 2, 3 and 4. Give a ball to player number 1.

- Tell the children to form a square, about two metres apart.

- 1 passes the ball to 2, who passes to 3, who passes to 4, who passes back to 1.

- Practise this a few times to ensure the children know the correct order.

- Next, tell the children to move around the area, still passing the ball in the same order. They cannot move when they are holding the ball.

- Repeat the activity with the children bouncing the ball to each other.

- Ask the children, 'How many passes can you make in a minute?'

Suggested space Hall or outside space

Learning outcomes To work on receiving a ball; to move in a controlled way around other children.

Resources One size 4 ball per group. A stopwatch.

Health and safety Ensure the receiver is looking at you before you throw the ball.

Be aware of other groups when moving around.

Simplification Use a larger ball and perform the activity standing still. Alternatively, the children could roll the ball instead of throwing it.

Extension Set a challenge to see how many passes the group can make in 30 seconds or a minute. Use a smaller ball and tell the children they can only make one-handed catches.

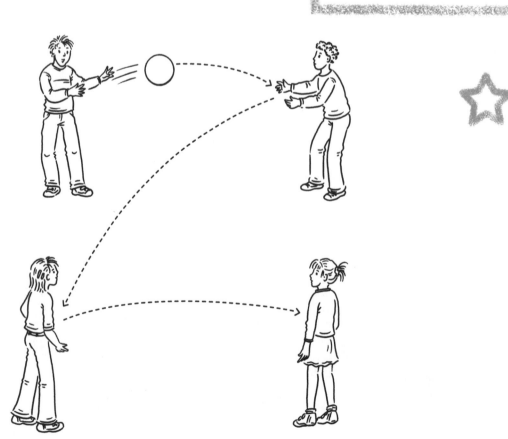

Hoops 'R' Us

- Ask the children to join hands in a large circle. Introduce the hoop to the circle, and from this point everyone's hands must remain joined.

- The objective of the activity is to move the hoop around the circle without breaking the chain.

- Tell the children they have to decide how they are going to manoeuvre their body through the hoop.

- If they are having problems, you could suggest that they use their feet first and move the hoop upwards, or put their head through first and move the hoop downwards.

- The children need to work together to ensure that the hoop continues its path around the circle.

- If anyone breaks the chain, that child has to run once around the circle before rejoining the group (this is only possible if space allows).

Suggested space Hall, outside space or classroom

Learning outcomes To work together cooperatively; to use communication effectively to complete the task; to gain an awareness of the body and its range of movements.

Resources One medium sized hoop

Health and safety Make sure there is enough room for the children to take large steps and swing their arms.

Simplification Use a larger hoop, or split the children into smaller groups of approximately 6–8.

Extension Use a smaller hoop or use more than one hoop, each going in a different direction.

Teamwork and cooperation

Crocodiles and Alligators

- Ask the children to get into groups of about six and give each group four sequencing spots or small mats.

- Tell the groups to line up on one side of the hall.

- Each group has to travel from one side of the hall to the other only by standing on the sequencing spots. If anyone steps off, the crocodiles and alligators eat them and they are out of the exercise.

- Give the children a few minutes to plan how they are going to achieve the task and practise. Remind them that they will have to work together to complete the task.

Suggested space Hall

Learning outcomes To work together cooperatively to complete a task; to work as a team to solve a problem; to experience balancing on a small area.

Resources Four sequencing spots or small gym mats per group of six

Health and safety Make sure the mats are light enough to be lifted by the children.

Simplification Use larger mats and explain how the task should be completed, or reduce the size of the area to be covered.

Extension Use smaller or fewer mats, or increase the size of the area to be covered.

Hot Potato

- Put the children into mixed ability groups of 6–8 and give a ball to one child in each group.

- Ask each group to stand in a circle with about one metre between children.

- On your signal, the child with the ball passes to the next person in the circle in a clockwise direction. The aim of the game is for the next person to catch the ball and pass it on.

- If anyone drops the ball, they have to run around the circle and try to 'beat the ball' back to their space; the other children continue to pass the ball and try to beat the runner.

- On your signal, the ball changes direction and the children pass it in an anti-clockwise direction.

- Ask the children, 'How can you make sure you are prepared to catch the ball?' and 'Why do you sometimes drop the ball?'

Suggested space Outside space

Learning outcomes To work cooperatively as a team; to examine what is needed to catch with consistency.

Resources One size 4 ball per group of 6–8

Health and safety Ensure that there is enough room for children to run around the outside of each circle.

Simplification Reduce the distance between the children in the circle. Use a larger ball.

Extension Change the type of ball being used, for example use a rugby ball. Increase the amount of space between the children in the circle. Vary the type of throw used.

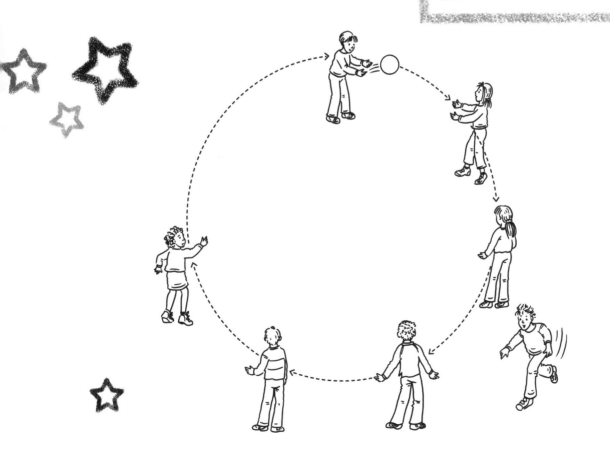

Find the Set

- Split the children into four teams and give each team a category (see 'Resources', right).

- Ask each team to line up at one end of the hall, behind their coloured marker.

- Spread the name cards out face down at the other end of the hall. Space them out randomly.

- The children have to run up individually (one from each team at a time) and turn over one card each, looking for a name from their category. If they find one, they pick it up and run back to their team and the next child runs up to the cards.

- If the card isn't from their category, they turn it back over, run back to their team and the next child then runs out.

- Team members can communicate with each other to help turn over the correct cards.

- Each child can only turn over one card per turn.

- The winning team is the first one to get all the cards in their category back to their coloured marker.

- Ask the children, 'How did you know which card to turn over?' and 'Did you work out a strategy with your team before you started?'

Suggested space Hall (or outside space if it's dry and there's no wind).

Learning outcomes To work together cooperatively; to use communication effectively.

Resources Four coloured cones or markers. Approximately 24 name cards, six from each category (categories could include planets, fruits, colours and sports).

Health and safety Make sure you look ahead when running.

Simplification Use pictures on the cards instead of words.

Extension Ask the teams to work out a strategy before starting the task.

keep the Order

- Split the class into groups of about six (each group could have more or fewer children depending on class size).

- Ask each group to stand in a circle, spaced out so they cannot quite hold hands.

- Give one child in each group a koosh ball. He/she has to throw it to another child in their circle (not the child to either side).

- That child throws it to another child, and so on until everyone in the group has caught the ball once.

- Repeat the activity, with the ball going to each child in the same order as before.

- Once the group is familiar with the pattern, add another piece of equipment in addition to the koosh ball (a large ball or a hoop – these should be rolled). This piece of equipment follows the same order.

- Once the group can manage this, add the third piece of equipment.

- Ask the children, 'How did you remember the set order?' and 'Which piece of equipment was the hardest to control?'

Suggested space Hall or outside space

Learning outcomes To work as a group to establish a set pattern; to look at various ways of sending and receiving an object.

Resources Five hoops, five koosh balls and five large balls

Health and safety Ensure there is plenty of space for each group.

Simplification Use only one piece of equipment – this could be a large ball.

Extension Put all the groups together in one large circle. Each group has to stick to its pattern, so there will be several pieces of equipment being passed around at the same time.

Teamwork and cooperation

Beat the Ball

- Set out a circuit the size of a netball court using the marker cones.

- Divide the group into two teams of equal number and name them A and B.

- Ask team A to line up along the side of the circuit and team B to line up one behind the other in the middle of the circuit.

- Give the ball to the first child in team A. On your command of 'Go!' he/she throws the ball as far as he/she can, then runs around the circuit back to the starting point.

- The children in team B fetch the ball and then get back into line with their legs apart.

- The child at the front of the line takes the ball and passes or rolls it through everybody's legs until it arrives at the child at the back of the line, who holds it up in the air.

- If the runner beats the ball, team A gets a point; if team B holds the ball in the air before the runner gets back to the starting point, team B gets a point.

- After everyone in team A has had a go at throwing and running, ask the teams to swap over. The winner is the team with the most points at the end of the game.

Suggested space Outside space

Learning outcomes To work cooperatively within a team; to use speed along with teamwork to complete a task.

Resources A large soft ball; four marker cones

Health and safety Be careful not to bump your head when you bend forwards to put the ball between your legs – make sure you have enough room.

Simplification Make the circuit larger or smaller depending on whether a team is finding it easy to get around and beat the ball or not.

Extension Feed the ball for the children to hit with a racket instead of asking them to throw it.

Active Every Day: Lower Key Stage 2 © Linda Kelly and Wendy Seward 2006, A & C Black Publishers Ltd

Steal the Treasure

- Place one hoop in the centre of the playing area and put all the bean bags (the 'treasure') inside it.

- Put one hoop in each corner of the playing area, away from the sides or walls and an equal distance from the centre hoop.

- Divide the children into four teams and ask each team to stand by one of the hoops. This is their base.

- When you say 'Go!' one member from each team has to run out to the centre hoop and collect a bean bag, then run back and put it in their base hoop. Then the next child from each team runs; this continues until all the bean bags have gone from the centre hoop.

- Runners can then go to one of the other teams' base hoops and 'steal' a bean bag to put back in their hoop.

- Stop the game at any time and count up the bean bags in each of the base hoops to find the winning team.

- Ask the children, 'Which team did you steal treasure from?' and 'Why did you choose that team?'

Suggested space Hall or outside space

Learning outcomes To work together as a team to achieve an outcome; to work out a strategy for being successful.

Resources Five hoops; about 30 bean bags

Health and safety Ensure that only one child from each team is running at a time.

Simplification Stop the game when all the bean bags have gone from the middle hoop.

Extension The children can choose to go for the middle hoop or can steal from the other teams' hoops straight away.

Teamwork and cooperation

Number Challenge

- Ask the children to sit down cross-legged in a large circle. Number the children 1–6 around the circle (starting at number 1 again for the seventh child).

- Put the bean bag in the centre of the circle.

- When you call out a number, all the children with that number have to get up and hop clockwise around the circle.

- Tell them to hop on their right leg for five hops, then change to their left leg for five hops and so on.

- When the children get back to their starting places, they go through the gap into the circle and try to pick up the bean bag.

- Whoever picks up the bean bag replaces it and calls out the next number – remind them that they can't call out their own number.

Suggested space Hall or outside space

Learning outcomes To remember and follow a command; to work safely and cooperatively with the rest of the class; to increase levels of fitness and awareness.

Resources One bean bag

Health and safety Tell the children that they must stay on their feet when attempting to pick up the bean bag and should not overtake when running around the circle.

Simplification Ask the children to run only as far as their original place in the circle, without retrieving the bean bag.

Extension Call out 'even numbers' or 'odd numbers' so half the group runs at once. If the group is mathematically able, you could ask for 'multiples of three' and so on.

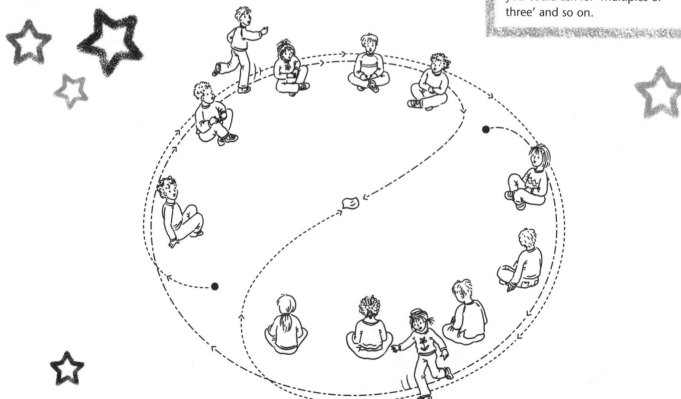

Active Every Day: Lower Key Stage 2 © Linda Kelly and Wendy Seward 2006, A & C Black Publishers Ltd

Tops 'n' Tails

- Tell half the class that they are 'tops' and the other half that they are 'tails'.

- Give each child a coloured marker and ask them to find a space in the playing area.

- Ask each child to place their marker on the floor depending on their given name, so the 'tops' place their marker the right way round (with the large base touching the floor) and the 'tails' place their marker upside-down (with the small area touching the floor).

- Tell the children that the objective of the game is to turn the opposing team's markers over so that 'tops' become 'tails' and vice versa. Players are not allowed to guard a marker or return to the same marker until they have switched a further two over.

- Start the game with a command or a whistle.

- Stop after 30 seconds to check on the progress of the teams and discuss effective strategies for success.

- Restart the game and after two minutes compare the number of 'tops' to the number of 'tails'. Discuss strategies with the children again.

- You can now mix up the groups if desired and restart the game.

Suggested space Hall or outside space (around two-thirds of a netball court)

Learning outcomes To work together cooperatively; to use communication effectively; to increase levels of fitness and awareness.

Resources One coloured marker per child. Whistle if desired.

Health and safety Always look ahead when running and be aware of the other children around you.

Simplification Put the children into smaller groups of 6–8.

Extension Increase the size of the playing area, for example to half of a primary football pitch.

Teamwork and cooperation

Vegetable Soup

- Ask the children to sit cross-legged in a large circle.

- Go around the circle giving every child in turn the name of a vegetable. Use six vegetables so there are approximately four children to each vegetable. The vegetables could be:

  - potato
  - carrot
  - onion
  - parsnip
  - pea
  - turnip

- Call out a vegetable and the children with that name have to get up and run around the circle clockwise before returning to sit down in their place.

- If you call out 'Vegetable Soup' all the children get up and touch the four perimeter walls/fences/lines before returning to sit in their original place.

Suggested space Hall or outside space

Learning outcomes To remember and respond to a given name; to work cooperatively with the rest of the class; to experience short bursts of cardiovascular exercise.

Resources None

Health and safety Make sure there is no pushing or overtaking when pupils are running around the circle.

Simplification Only use four different vegetables.

Extension Call out two or three vegetables at a time.

Shuttle Relays

- Set out the cones as follows:

    - cone 1: starting point

    - cone 2: 5 m ahead of cone 1

    - cone 3: 5 m ahead of cone 2

- Split the class into teams of approximately 4–6 children and ask each team to line up behind their starting cone.

- Tell the children to jog in relay formation (one starting after the other has finished) around the furthest cone and return to the starting point. Continue until all the children have had a go.

- Now change the drill to: sidestep to cone 2, jog around cone 3 and sidestep back from cone 2.

- The next drill could be: hop on your right foot to cone 2, jump with both feet together around cone 3 and hop back from cone 2 on your left foot.

- Continue in this way, using a mixture of jogging, hopping, jumping, sidestepping, hopscotch and so on.

- Ask the children, 'Which way of moving made you breathe faster?' and 'Why do you think that is?'

Suggested space Hall or outside space

Learning outcomes To examine what type of exercises make you breathe harder; to follow a set of instructions to complete a task; to increase levels of fitness and awareness.

Resources Three marker cones per team

Health and safety Ensure there is enough room between the groups.

Simplification Remove the second cone and ask the children to do the same action for the whole drill.

Extension Make the drill instructions more complicated so that each cone initiates a new way of moving. For example, 'sidestep to cone 2, jog to cone 3, hop back to cone 2 and jump with feet together back to cone 1'.

Stamina, speed and agility

Roller Ball

- Ask half of the class to make a large circle and the other half of the class to stand inside the circle.

- Roll the ball into the circle, making sure that it stays on the floor.

- If the ball hits any of the children inside the circle below the knee, they are out and join the group who are forming the circle.

- Whoever receives the ball on the opposite side of the circle rolls it back in, again aiming to hit the children inside the circle below the knee.

- Tell the children inside the circle that they will have to react quickly to avoid the moving ball from hitting them.

- The last child left inside the circle is the winner.

- Restart the game with the other half of the class inside the circle (that is, the two groups swap roles).

- Ask the children, 'Why does this game make you breathe heavily?' and 'What do you do when you see the ball coming towards you?'

- You could add a second ball to increase awareness.

Suggested space Hall or outside space

Learning outcomes To examine the effect of a simple game on breathing; to improve agility and speed of reaction.

Resources One large soft ball

Health and safety Ensure that the children roll the ball and keep it below knee height.

Simplification Make the circle larger and ensure the ball is rolled very slowly. Ensure all pupils are looking at the ball when it is rolled.

Extension Use a smaller ball and make the circle smaller.

On the Road

- Ask the children to get into pairs and stand one behind the other in a space.

- Give the first child in each pair a sequencing spot to use as a steering wheel.

- Ask the children to move around the playing area, avoiding all other 'road' users.

- Call out the following commands for the children to follow:

  - 'Red'   Stop

  - 'Amber'   Jump on the spot

  - 'Green'   Go

  - 'Change driver'   Swap the child in front

  - 'Puncture'   Stop and lean out sideways into a stretch

  - 'Oil change'   Stop, stretch up on toes, turn and change direction.

- When the children are on 'Green', call out gear changes, starting slowly and building up speed:

  - 'Slowly start'   A slow walk

  - 'Up a gear'   Marching pace

  - 'Slightly faster' A slow jog

  - 'Faster still'   A run

  - 'Reverse'   Move backwards

- Ask the children, 'Why does the car go through the gears before it gets faster?' and 'Which gear makes you the most out of breath?'

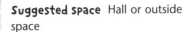

Stamina, speed and agility

Stuck in the Mud

- Choose a few children to be 'on'. The rest of the class are 'free'. (In a class of 30, about 5 should be 'on' and 25 should be 'free'.)

- Tell the 'free' children to run around the playing area, trying to avoid the children who are 'on'. The players who are 'on' should try to tag the 'free' players.

- If a child is caught, he or she becomes 'stuck in the mud' and has to stand still with his/her arms stretched out wide.

- The only way to free a child who has been caught is if a 'free' child (who is not 'stuck') moves under his/her arms.

- Stop the game at any time to discuss the effectiveness of the strategies used.

Suggested space Hall or playground

Learning outcomes To increase levels of agility and awareness.

Resources A set of bands to show which children are 'on'.

Health and safety Take care when going under other people's arms.

Simplification Have a larger number of children 'on'.

Extension Increase the size of the playing area or have fewer children 'on'.

Active Every Day: Lower Key Stage 2 © Linda Kelly and Wendy Seward 2006, A & C Black Publishers Ltd

keep it Moving

- Set out the cones in a large circle (as large as the playing area allows) and number the cones 1–7.

- Divide the class into equal teams with about eight children in each team. Number the children in each team 1–8.

- Ask the children to stand by the cone that matches their number, so child 1 stands at cone 1 and so on. The children numbered 8 should stand at cone 1.

- Each cone should therefore have the same number of children standing by it as the number of teams involved, except cone 1 which will have double.

- Give all the number 1 children a bean bag.

- The number 1 children start the activity by running to the next cone, where they pass the bean bag to the next person in their team. The number 2 children then continue the drill by running on to the next cone and passing the bean bag to the number 3 children, and so on around the circle. When the number 8 children get the bean bag, they continue the drill by running to cone number 2 and passing to the number 1 children. Remind the children that they should stay at their cones until the bean bag comes around to them.

- When all the children are back to their original starting places and the bean bag has travelled around the circle seven times, the activity is over.

- At first, the children can perform the activity at a jog, then start running faster once they have the hang of it.

- Ask the children, 'Which type of running made you breathe faster?' and 'Which activity used speed and which used stamina?'

Suggested space Hall or outside space

Learning outcomes To work cooperatively as a team to achieve the desired outcome; to examine the differences between speed and stamina; to improve levels of fitness and awareness.

Resources One fewer cone than the number in a team (so if you have teams of eight you need seven cones); one bean bag per team

Health and safety Make sure there is enough room for all the teams to run and pass the bean bag.

Simplification Have a smaller number of children in each team, for example four.

Extension Ask the children to move in different ways for each lap, for example sidesteps, jumps, hopscotch and so on.

Stamina, speed and agility

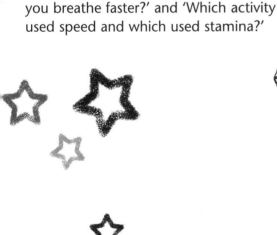

Cone Ball

- Arrange the children into groups of six.

- Use the cones to mark out a square with sides of 3–4 metres for each group. Place the three tennis balls on any of the cones (one should be left vacant).

- Ask the first child to take a tennis ball from one of the cones and move it to the vacant space, then move another tennis ball to the newly vacant space, and so on until each of the three balls has been moved.

- Each child in the group performs the activity until the group has completed the task.

- Each time, one child uses the stopwatch to time the activity. At the end, they can see which child was the quickest.

- Ask the children, 'Did you use a strategy to do the task?' and (where relevant) 'How did you do the task so quickly?' or 'What could you do to perform the task more quickly next time?'

Suggested space Hall or playground

Learning outcomes To increase levels of agility and awareness; to have responsibility for timing an activity.

Resources Three tennis balls and four marker cones per group; one stopwatch per group

Health and safety Make sure the playing surface is dry to prevent the children slipping, as they will be running and turning quickly.

Simplification Reduce the number of cones and balls used.

Extension Increase the distance between the cones.

Breathe Hard, Breathe Easy

- Ask the children to space out, facing you, with enough room to swing their arms.

- Ask the children to start off by walking on the spot.

- After one minute, increase the pace by asking them to march on the spot.

- After one minute, increase the pace to a jog on the spot.

- After another minute, tell them to go back to walking on the spot. Ask them 'Did your breathing get faster as the activity got faster?'

- After a minute of walking, ask the children to do star jumps for 20 seconds, followed by sprinting on the spot for 20 seconds, and then another 20 seconds of star jumps.

- Next, tell them to go back to walking on the spot for a minute. Ask them 'Did your breathing change when you were doing the star jumps and sprint?'

- Bring the activity to a close by asking the children to jog on the spot for a minute, then march on the spot for a minute and finally walk on the spot for a minute.

- You can ask the children more questions about how their breathing goes slowly back to normal as the exercise gets slower and easier.

Suggested space Hall, outside space or a classroom (if big enough)

Learning outcomes To experience how breathing goes up and down as exercises get harder; to raise levels of fitness and awareness.

Resources A stopwatch

Health and safety Make sure there is enough room for the children to perform star jumps.

Simplification Perform each activity for a shorter amount of time, for example 10 seconds for the exercises and 30 seconds for the marching and jogging.

Extension Include more activities such as 'touch the floor then jump up'.

Stamina, speed and agility

Feel the Beat

- Divide the class into teams of approximately 4–6 children.

- Give each team two marker cones. Ask half of the team to line up behind one cone at one side of the allocated space and the other half of the team to line up behind the second marker, approximately 10 metres away.

- Before starting, ask the children to measure their breathing rate by placing one hand on their tummy and one on their chest. Time 10 seconds and ask the children to count how many times their chest rises in that time, then remember this number.

- Ask the children to start by walking briskly one by one in a relay formation. This should last for about one minute.

- Next, ask them to increase their speed to a slow jog, again for about a minute.

- Next, call out 'fast jog', 'sidesteps', 'small jumps', 'hops' or 'hopscotch'. The children follow your command, keeping in relay order, until each child has done each activity a couple of times.

- Ask the children to measure their breathing rate again and compare it to their original rate.

- Finish the activity by asking the children to complete a few lengths with a slow jog and finally a walk. Finally, ask the children to measure their breathing rate again.

- Ask the children, 'Was there any change to your breathing rate? and 'What made it go up and come down?'

Suggested space Hall or outside space

Learning outcomes To experience how breathing gets faster with exercise; to work co-operatively as a team; to improve levels of fitness and awareness.

Resources Two marker cones per team.

Health and safety Ensure there is enough space between the groups.

Simplification Don't include as many changes.

Extension Include more complex activities such as moving backwards, cross-steps and so on.

Active Every Day: Lower Key Stage 2 © Linda Kelly and Wendy Seward 2006, A & C Black Publishers Ltd

Make a Chain

- This is a game of 'tag' with a difference.

- Select three children to be 'it' and ask them to chase the rest of the class.

- Once a child who is 'it' has tagged another child, those two children join hands. They then have to chase the other children while holding hands.

- If the pair of children tag a third child, all three have to join hands and continue to chase the other children.

- Once a fourth child has been tagged, the chasers split into two pairs and carry on chasing.

- The last three children to be tagged start as 'it' for the next game.

- Ask the children, 'Are you using speed, stamina, strength or flexibility in this game?'

Suggested space Hall or outside space

Learning outcomes To work cooperatively; to use speed and stamina in a simple game situation; to increase levels of fitness and awareness.

Resources None

Health and safety Discuss safety points about running when holding hands with someone else – the children need to take care not to swing each other around.

Simplification Only allow a maximum of two pupils to be joined together.

Extension Increase the size of the playing area.

Stamina, speed and agility

Through the Legs

- Ask the children to get into groups of six and stand one behind the other in a line with their legs apart. Place a marker cone at the start of each line.

- Give a ball to the child at the head of each line.

- On your signal, he or she aims and gently throws the ball back between the legs of the rest of the group.

- The child at the back of the group should be waiting, crouched down and hands ready to collect the ball after it has travelled through everyone's legs.

- Once the child at the back of the group has the ball, he/she should run to the front of the line and stand at the marker.

- Meanwhile, the rest of the group need to shuffle back to make space for the child with the ball to start at the marker.

- The new lead member now aims and gently throws the ball back between the legs of the rest of the group; again, the child at the end of the line collects the ball and runs to the front while the rest of the group shuffle back.

- Once each member of the group has played the part of lead member, the activity is over. (NB You may need to make adjustments to this if there are uneven groups – in smaller groups, one or two children may need to be lead member twice.)

- You can repeat the activity with the children passing the ball overhead.

Suggested space Hall or playground

Learning outcomes To increase levels of agility and awareness; to roll a ball with accuracy.

Resources A large ball (a size 4 netball or similar); one marker cone per group of six

Health and safety Ensure there is enough space between the children to prevent them bumping their heads when bending forwards.

Simplification Ask the children to pass the ball to each other along the line.

Extension Ask the children to pass the ball alternately overhead and through the legs.

Them Bones

- Ask the children to stand away from their desks in a space.

- Teach them the rhyme a line at a time, showing them the actions as you go.

- You can either speak or sing the rhyme.

(chorus)

(ask the children to walk around the room)
Them bones them bones gonna walk around
Them bones them bones gonna walk around
Them bones them bones gonna walk around
Walk around all day.

(ask the children to touch the bone that is named)
Well the foot bone's connected to the ankle bone
And the ankle bone's connected to the leg bone
And the leg bone's connected to the knee bone
And they walk around all day.

(repeat chorus)

(ask the children to touch the bone that is named)
Well the knee bone's connected to the thigh bone
And the thigh bone's connected to the hip bone
And the hip bone's connected to the back bone
And they walk around all day.

(repeat chorus)

(ask the children to touch the bone that is named)
Well the back bone's connected to the shoulder bone
And the shoulder bone's connected to the neck bone
And the neck bone's connected to the head bone
And they walk around all day.

(repeat chorus)

Suggested space Classroom

Learning outcomes To relate movements and actions to singing and verse; to remember a sequence of movements and actions.

Resources None

Health and safety Ensure that the children have enough space to perform the actions.

Action rhymes

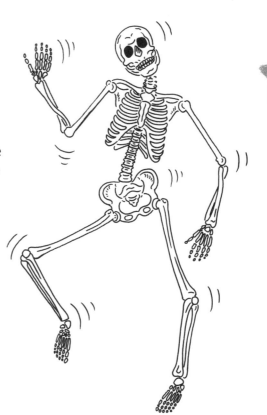

A Sailor Went to Sea

- Ask the children to stand away from their desks in a space.

- Teach them the rhyme a line at a time, showing them the actions as you go.

- You can either speak or sing the rhyme.

(chorus)

A sailor went to sea sea sea *(move your hands like waves on the sea)*
To see what he could see see see *(put your hands above your eyes as if you were looking out to sea)*
But all that he could see see see *(put your hands above your eyes)*
Was the bottom of the deep blue sea sea sea. *(move your hands like waves on the sea)*

(every time you say Ireland, perform an Irish jig)
A sailor went to Ireland
To see what he could Ireland
But all that he could Ireland
Was the bottom of the deep blue Ireland.

(repeat chorus)

(every time you say Spain, move around in a flamenco dance style)
A sailor went to Spain
To see what he could Spain
But all that he could Spain
Was the bottom of the deep blue Spain.

(repeat chorus)

(every time you say Honolulu, sway from one side to the other with your arms outstretched as if you were doing a Hawaiian dance)
A sailor went to Honolulu.
To see what he could Honolulu
But all that he could Honolulu.
Was the bottom of the deep blue Honolulu.

(repeat chorus)

Suggested space Classroom

Learning outcomes To relate movements and actions to singing and verse; to remember a sequence of movements and actions.

Resources None

Health and safety Ensure that the children have enough space to perform the actions.

Simplification Perform the chorus only.

Extension Ask the children to develop their own movements to add to the rhyme.

Hokey Cokey

- Ask the children to stand away from their desks in a space, or to form a circle around the edge of the room if there's enough space.

- Teach them the rhyme a line at a time, showing them the actions as you go.

- You can either speak or sing the rhyme.

You put your right arm in

(extend your right arm in front of you)

Right arm out

(take your arm back to your body)

Right arm in

(extend your right arm in front of you)

Shake it all about

(shake your right arm in front of you)

Smoke goes up the chimney *(stretch up high)* and you turn around *(turn around)*

That's what it's all about.

Oh the Hokey Cokey *(swing your arms above your head like a 'Mexican wave')*

Oh the Hokey Cokey *(swing your arms above your head like a 'Mexican wave')*

Oh the Hokey Cokey *(swing your arms above your head like a 'Mexican wave')*

Knees bend, arms stretch ra! ra! ra! *(bend your knees, stretch up and clap three times)*

- Continue the rhyme using a different part of the body each time, for example left arm, right leg, left leg and so on.

- The children can stand in their own spaces, in circles in small groups or with the whole group in a large circle as space allows.

Suggested space Classroom

Learning outcomes To relate movements and actions to singing and verse; to remember a sequence of movements and actions.

Resources None

Health and safety Ensure that the children have enough room to perform the actions.

Simplification Perform the chorus only.

Extension Include more complicated actions, for example hops in and out, cross-legged jumps in and out and so on.

Action rhymes

I am a Music Man

- Ask the children to stand away from their desks in a space.

- Teach them the rhyme a line at a time, showing them the actions as you go.

- You can either speak or sing the rhyme.

    (you say or sing) I am a music man, I come from round your way, and I can play.
    (the children respond) What can you play?

    (you initiate and the children join in) I can play the piano, piano, piano
    I can play the piano, the pia-pia-no. *(pretend to play the piano)*

    (you) I am a music man, I come from round your way, and I can play.
    (children's response) What can you play?

    (you initiate and the children join in) I can play the violin, violin, violin
    I can play the violin, the vio-vio-lin. *(pretend to play the violin)*

- Include a variety of other instruments, for example big bass drum, air guitar and so on.

- You could also adapt the words to a sporting theme, for example:

    (you) I am a sporting fan, I come from round your way, and I can play.
    (response) What can you play?

    (you initiate and the children join in) I can play football, football, football *(pretend to be kicking a ball)* and so on.

Suggested space Classroom

Learning outcomes To relate movements and actions to singing and verse; to remember a sequence of movements and actions.

Resources None

Health and safety Ensure that the children have enough room to perform the actions.

Extension Ask the children to suggest different instruments and demonstrate the accompanying action.

If You're Happy and You know It

- Ask the children to stand away from their desks in a space.

- Teach them the rhyme a verse at a time, showing them the appropriate action. The children should perform the action mentioned in each verse (so in verse 1 they clap their hands, in verse 2 they stamp their feet and so on).

- You can either speak or sing the rhyme.

If you're happy and you know it clap your hands
If you're happy and you know it clap your hands
If you're happy and you know it and you really want to
    show it
If you're happy and you know it clap your hands.

If you're happy and you know it stamp your feet
If you're happy and you know it stamp your feet
If you're happy and you know it and you really want to
    show it
If you're happy and you know it stamp your feet.

Verse 3: use 'turn around' as the words and action.

Verse 4: use 'touch the ground' as the words and action.

If you're happy and you know it say 'we are!'
If you're happy and you know it say 'we are!'
If you're happy and you know it and you really want to
    show it
If you're happy and you know it say 'we are!'

Suggested space Classroom

Learning outcomes To relate movements and actions to singing and verse; to remember a sequence of movements and actions.

Resources None

Health and safety Ensure that the children have enough room to perform the activity.

Extension Ask the children to suggest alternative actions for the verses.

Action rhymes

Jack and Jill

● Ask the children to stand away from their desks in a space.

● Teach them the rhyme a line at a time, showing them the actions as you go.

Jack and Jill went off to France

(the children march on the spot)

To teach the ladies a hula dance

(the children move their arms from side to side)

Swinging hips both to and fro

(the children continue the arm movements and swing their hips from side to side)

Swinging high and swinging low

(the children continue the movement, moving their arms up and down)

Up and down and round and round

(the children continue moving as before and include a couple of turns on the spot)

Stretch up high then touch the ground

(the children stretch up high and then touch the ground)

Hula left and hula right

(the children perform the hula action to the left and right)

Hula dancing through the night!

(the children perform the hula action and finish with a turn and a stretch)

Suggested space Classroom

Learning outcomes To relate movements and actions to verse; to remember a sequence of movements and actions.

Resources None

Health and safety Ensure that the children have enough room to perform the activity.

Simplification Modify the actions to make them easier if some children are struggling.

Extension Ask the children to perform more complex movements. For example, they could imagine they were travelling to France using different forms of transport (train, car) or develop the hula dance to include turns and height differences.

Active Every Day: Lower Key Stage 2 © Linda Kelly and Wendy Seward 2006, A & C Black Publishers Ltd

January to December

- Ask the children to stand away from their desks in a space.

- Teach them the rhyme a line at a time, showing them the actions as you go.

January brings the snow, throwing snowballs high and low

(the children pretend to gather snow, roll it into a ball and throw it)

February brings the ice, skate and slide it's very nice

(the children pretend to skate around the room)

March brings flowers breaking through

(the children imagine they are flowers just breaking through the ground and growing into full bloom)

April showers wet me and you

(the children hop around, pretending to avoid raindrops)

May is windy, jump around

(the children jump around, changing direction)

June is lovely, touch the ground

(the children jump around and touch the ground)

In July skip on the spot

(the children skip on the spot)

In August marching is your lot

(the children march around the room)

A September walk is nice and slow

(the children walk slowly around the room, changing direction)

October's faster, off you go

(the children increase their speed to a jog)

Race through November, it's almost clear

(the children increase their speed still further)

Slow down and stop, December's here!

(the children stop and rest).

Suggested space Hall or outside space

Learning outcomes To relate movements and actions to singing and verse; to remember a sequence of movements and actions.

Resources None

Health and safety Ensure that the children have enough room to perform the actions; remind the children that they need to look around them when running.

Action rhymes

Old Macdonald

- Ask the children to stand away from their desks in a space.

- Teach them the rhyme a verse at a time, showing them the actions as you go.

- In this song, the actions only come once the adjectives are used: big, little, fat and thin.

Old Macdonald had a farm, ee-i ee-i oh
And on that farm he had some cows, ee-i ee-i oh
There were big cows, little cows, little cows, big cows

Fat cows, thin cows, thin cows, fat cows

*(for 'big' lift one arm up and the other one down
for 'little' bring both hands close together
for 'fat' stretch your arms wide
for 'thin' bring your hands close together)*

Old Macdonald had a farm, ee-i ee-i oh.

Old Macdonald had a farm, ee-i ee-i oh
And on that farm he had some pigs, ee-i ee-i oh
There were big pigs, little pigs, little pigs, big pigs
Fat pigs, thin pigs, thin pigs, fat pigs
Big cows, little cows, little cows, big cows
Fat cows, thin cows, thin cows, fat cows
Old Macdonald had a farm, ee-i ee-i oh.

Verse 3: include sheep to go with the pigs and cows.

Verse 4: include ducks to go with the sheep, pigs and cows.

Suggested space Classroom

Learning outcomes To relate movements and actions to singing; to remember a sequence of movements and actions.

Resources None

Health and safety Ensure that the children have enough room to perform the activity.

Active Every Day: Lower Key Stage 2 © Linda Kelly and Wendy Seward 2006, A & C Black Publishers Ltd

Ten in the Bed

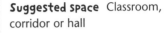

- Ask the children to stand away from their desks in a space.

- Teach them the rhyme a verse at a time, showing them the actions as you go.

There were ten in the bed and the little one said roll over, roll over *(the children turn around whenever they say 'roll over')*
So they all rolled over *(the children turn around)* and one fell out *(the children crouch down and touch the floor)* and he landed on the floor with a bump and a shout *(the children sit down)*
Please remember when you are rising early *(the children stand up from floor)*
Please remember when you get out of bed *(the children jump on the spot)*
Please remember to tie the cord in your pyjamas *(the children mime a tying action, ending with their arms outstretched to the sides)*
Single beds are only made for one, two, three, four, five, six, seven, eight, nine *(the children clap as they say each number)*

Repeat the song with the numbers going down, so:

There were nine in the bed and the little one said roll over, roll over
So they all rolled over and one fell out and he landed on the floor with a bump and a shout
Please remember when you are rising early, please remember when you get out of bed
Please remember to tie the cord in your pyjamas, single beds are only made for one, two, three, four, five, six, seven, eight

There were eight in the bed and the little one said roll over, roll over etc.

Continue until there is only one in the bed.

Suggested space Classroom, corridor or hall

Learning outcomes To relate movements and actions to singing and verse; to remember a sequence of movements and actions.

Resources None

Health and safety Ensure that the children have enough room to perform the activity.

Simplification Adapt the activities to suit individuals.

Extension Increase the level of activity.

Action rhymes

Tennis, Football, Ski and Skate!

- Note: this is a variation of the old favourite 'Head, Shoulders, Knees and Toes'.

- Ask the children to stand away from their desks in a space.

- Teach them the rhyme a verse at a time, showing them the actions as you go.

- To the beat of 'Head, Shoulders, Knees and Toes', sing 'Tennis, Football, Ski and Skate, Ski and Skate'.

- As each sport is mentioned, everyone mimes the action of that sport.

- As with the original song, in each verse you leave out one more activity, but still perform the action. So, verse two is '. . ., football, ski and skate'; verse three is '. . ., . . ., ski and skate' and so on.

- The penultimate verse of the song should therefore only include the actions – no singing at all.

- The final verse should be a repeat of the first verse, with all the actions and words together.

Suggested space Classroom

Learning outcome To copy and repeat a short exercise.

Resources None

Health and safety Ensure that the children have enough room to perform the actions.

Simplification Perform the activity as simply 'Head, shoulders, knees and toes, knees and toes'.

Extension Ask the children to make up their own version of the song and lead the rest of the group. Increase the speed of the activity.

50

Teddy Bear, Teddy Bear

● Arrange the children into groups with a maximum of eight children per group.

● Teach the children the rhyme and actions a line at a time and make sure they all know it before starting to skip.

● Give each group a long skipping rope. The children take it in turns to turn the rope in pairs, one holding each end.

● Ask all of the children to chant the rhyme together. One child jumps at a time, jumping in before the rhyme starts and jumping out at the end.

Teddy bear, teddy bear, touch the ground *(the child touches the ground)*
Teddy bear, teddy bear, turn around *(the child turns around)*
Teddy bear, teddy bear, walk upstairs *(the child jumps along the rope as it is moving)*
Teddy bear, teddy bear, say your prayers *(the child puts his/her hands together or makes another suitable religious gesture)*
Teddy bear, teddy bear, do the splits *(the child does a star jump)*
Teddy bear, teddy bear, do high kicks *(kick once with each leg)*
Teddy bear, teddy bear, turn out the light *(the child prepares to jump out)*
Teddy bear, teddy bear, say good night *(the child jumps out of the rope and waves)*

● Repeat until all of the children, including the rope turners, have had a turn.

Suggested space Outside space

Learning outcomes To use skipping to improve stamina and fitness levels; to remember and repeat a rhyme.

Resources Long skipping ropes (one per group with a maximum of eight children per group)

Health and safety Ensure that the children have enough room to perform the activity.

Skipping

Skipping Challenges

- Give each child a skipping rope and ask them to find a space in the playing area.

- Ask them to perform a few simple skips to warm up, skipping both forwards and backwards.

- Skip for a count of ten (counting the skips).

- Rest for a count of ten.

- Skip for a count of twenty.

- Rest for a count of twenty.

- Next, ask the children to find a partner, stand facing each other and skip using just one rope, which one of the pair turns.

- Practise this paired skipping until the pairs are confident they are both skipping at the same time.

- Skip together for a count of ten (counting the skips).

- Rest for a count of ten.

- Skip together for a count of twenty.

- Rest for a count of twenty.

Suggested space Hall or outside space

Learning outcomes To use skipping to improve stamina and fitness levels; to work cooperatively with a partner to achieve an outcome.

Resources One skipping rope per child

Health and safety Make sure that the children get enough rest, as outlined in the activity. Ensure that the children have enough room to perform the activity.

Extension Ask the children to try skipping backwards with a partner.

52

Spanish Dancer

- Arrange the children into groups with a maximum of eight children per group.

- Give each group a long skipping rope. The children take it in turns to turn the rope in pairs, one holding each end.

- Ask all of the children to chant the rhyme together.

Not last night but the night before
Twenty-four robbers came knocking at the door
They called me out for the world to see *(the first child jumps into the rope and continues to jump, performing the actions in the rhyme)*
And this is what they said to me
Spanish dancer, turn around *(the child turns around)*
Spanish dancer, touch the ground *(the child touches the ground)*
Spanish dancer, do high kicks *(the child kicks the left leg then the right leg)*
Spanish dancer, do the splits. *(the child does a star jump)*
(the child then jumps out and the next child gets ready to jump in as the rhyme starts again from the beginning)

- Continue until all of the children have had a turn, including the rope turners.

Skipping

Cross-overs

- Give each child a skipping rope and ask them to find a space in the playing area.

- Ask them to warm up with some basic skips, both forwards and backwards.

- First, ask them to cross and uncross their legs on every alternate jump and continue skipping, making sure they alternate the leg that goes in front.

- Go back to basic skipping, both forwards and backwards.

- Next, ask them to keep hold of the rope and continue turning it as they cross their arms in front of their body. They now skip through the loop in the rope that they have made by crossing their arms.

- After two crosses, they can uncross their arms to skip normally.

- Continue, alternating crossed and uncrossed arms on each skip.

Suggested space Hall or outside space

Learning outcomes To use skipping to improve stamina and fitness levels; to coordinate the turning of the rope with the actions.

Resources One skipping rope per child

Health and safety Ensure that the children have enough room to perform the activity successfully.

Simplification Set simpler targets for children who are struggling.

Extension Ask the children to try turning the rope backwards.

All in Together, Guys!

- Arrange the children into groups with a maximum of eight children per group.

- Give each group a long skipping rope. The children take it in turns to turn the rope in pairs, one holding each end.

- Ask all of the children to chant the rhyme together.

- For the first verse, the children jump in to the rope when their birthday month is named, and carry on jumping until December.

- For the second verse, the children jump out of the rope when their birthday month is named.

All in together, guys
How do you like the weather, guys?
When it is your birthday, please jump in!
January, February, March, April, May, June, July, August,
September, October, November, December.

All in together, guys
How do you like the weather guys?
When it is your birthday, please jump out!
January, February, March, April, May, June, July, August,
September, October, November, December.

- Continues until all the players have had a go at turning the rope.

Skipping

Jumping Jacks

- Give each child a skipping rope and ask them to find a space in the playing area.

- Ask the children to perform a few simple skips, both forwards and backwards, to warm up.

- Next, ask the children to jump their feet out to shoulder-width apart and bring back together while they skip.

- Repeat this several times until they are all confident in doing this.

- Now, give the children number patterns to follow. For example, 'three – two' means three jumps with their legs wide and two jumps with their legs together, and 'four – six' means four jumps with their legs wide and six jumps with their legs together.

- Rest and repeat.

Suggested space Hall or outside space

Learning outcomes To use skipping to improve stamina and fitness levels; to practise and improve levels of coordination.

Resources One skipping rope per child

Health and safety Ensure that the children have enough room to perform the activity; make sure that the children rest every few minutes.

Two Little Dickie Birds

- Arrange the children into groups with a maximum of eight children per group.

- Give each group a long skipping rope. The children take it in turns to turn the rope in pairs, one holding each end.

- The rope turners chant the rhyme together as they turn the rope.

Two little dickie birds sitting on a wall
(two children jump in to the turning rope)
One named . . ., one named . . .

(each child calls out his/her name in turn and waves)
Fly away . . ., fly away . . .

(the rope turners call out the jumpers' names and the children jump out as their name is called)

Come back . . ., come back . . .
(the children jump back in as their name is called)
Now fly away, fly away, fly away all.
(both children jump out)

- Continue until everyone has had a turn, including the rope turners.

Suggested space Outside space

Learning outcomes To use skipping to improve stamina and fitness levels; to remember and repeat a rhyme.

Resources Long skipping ropes (one per group with a maximum of eight children per group)

Health and safety Ensure that the children have enough room to perform the activity.

Skipping

Scissor Jumps

- Give each child a skipping rope and ask them to stand in a space in the playing area.

- Ask them to perform a few simple skips, both forwards and backwards, to warm up.

- Next, ask them to jump with one foot forwards and one foot back for one skip, then go back to normal skipping.

- Repeat this several times until they are confident in doing this.

- Now, ask them to do the same action but with the other foot forwards. Repeat until they are confident with this.

- Finally, ask them to skip with alternate feet forward in a 'spotty dog' action.

- Rest and repeat.

Suggested space Hall or outside space

Learning outcomes To use skipping to improve stamina and fitness levels; to improve coordination and control.

Resources One skipping rope per child

Health and safety Ensure that the children have enough room to perform the activity.

Going to a Party

- Give each child a skipping rope and ask them to find a space in the playing area.

- The children chant the rhyme as they skip.

Going to a party, don't know what to wear
Spilled a drink on my new clothes and now I'm in despair!

How many seconds did I cry?
1, 2, 3, 4 and so on *(the children count how many skips they can do)*

- Rest, then repeat. Ask the children to try to beat their previous score.

- Repeat with the children skipping backwards

- Repeat with the children using the cross-over rope technique (crossing their arms and skipping)

Suggested space Hall or outside space

Learning outcomes To use skipping to improve stamina and fitness levels; to remember and repeat a rhyme.

Resources One skipping rope per child

Health and safety Ensure that the children have enough room to perform the activity.

Skipping

Skip Together

- Give each child a skipping rope and ask them to get into pairs.

- Ask each pair to stand side by side in a space in the playing area and start skipping, trying to skip in unison with each other.

- After practising this for a minute or so, ask the children to swap the ropes they are holding with their inside hands (the hand closest to their partner), so each child is holding one end of their partner's rope.

- Ask the children to try to carry on skipping.

- Set the children a target depending on how well they can perform this activity and see if they can beat that target.

- If the children are successful, ask them to try turning the rope backwards.

Suggested space Hall or outside space

Learning outcomes To use skipping to improve stamina and fitness levels; to work cooperatively with a partner.

Resources One skipping rope per child

Health and safety Ensure that children have enough room to perform the activity, especially when they are skipping side by side.

Simplification Set simple targets for individuals who are struggling.

Extension Ask the children to try to beat their best score.

Appendix: Checklists

Following are a number of forms for you to use in conjunction with the *Active Every Day* programme. One of these is simply a record sheet to remind you which activities you have used and on which you can record appropriate comments. The other three forms are for use by the children and can be used at any time of year, either on their own or as part of a linked, cross-curricular project or themed week. The forms are:

1.   A questionnaire that will give you an insight into individual children's opinions of and attitudes to physical activity.

2.   A daily physical activity record sheet that will tell you the amount and range of physical activities that children participate in, both in and out of school. It also asks children to think about how exercise affects breathing patterns.

3.   A weekly physical activity record sheet that will tell you the amount and range of physical activities that children participate in, both in and out of school. It also asks the children a range of questions relating to activity patterns.

Attitudes to physical activity

Name _____

Date _____

Tick the box that fits how you feel about each sentence

	Always	Sometimes	Never
1. I enjoy physical activity			
2. I like exercising with others			
3. I like to exercise on my own			
4. I find physical exercise easy			
5. I find physical exercise hard			
6. I like to play games as part of a team			
7. I find throwing and catching difficult			
8. Running makes me out of breath			
9. I find it easy to remember rhymes and songs			
10. I take part in physical activity every day			

Daily physical activity record sheet

Name _____

Monday   Tuesday   Wednesday   Thursday   Friday   Saturday   Sunday

(Circle the correct day)

When?	What did you do?	Time spent in minutes?	How fast did it make you breathe? *(Circle the correct description)*
Before school			Very fast quite fast normal
Break/lunch time			Very fast quite fast normal
Lesson time			Very fast quite fast normal
After school			Very fast quite fast normal
Evening			Very fast quite fast normal

● Total time spent being active _____

● Did you manage to breathe fast for an hour?   Yes   No

● Can you describe to another person how your body felt during and after exercise?

Weekly physical activity diary

Name _____

Start date _____ End date _____

Day	What did you do?	How long did you do it for? *(in minutes)*	How fast did it make you breathe?
Monday am			
Monday pm			
Tuesday am			
Tuesday pm			
Wednesday am			
Wednesday pm			
Thursday am			
Thursday pm			
Friday am			
Friday pm			
Saturday am			
Saturday pm			
Sunday am			
Sunday pm			

Active Every Day: Lower Key Stage 2 © Linda Kelly and Wendy Seward 2006, A & C Black Publishers Ltd

Weekly physical activity diary

How many minutes of physical activity did you do during the week?

_____

How much physical activity did you do in the mornings?

_____

How much physical activity did you do in the afternoons?

_____

How many minutes of physical activity were done at school?

_____

Which activities made you breathe fast?

_____

Which activities allowed your breathing to stay normal?

_____

Did you do any physical activities that were new to you this week?

_____

Which was your favourite activity?

_____

Did you remember to drink plenty of water?

_____

What do you plan to do next week?

_____

Activity checklist

Theme	Activity	When used	Comments
Limited space	One, Two, Three		
Limited space	Sporting Heroes		
Limited space	Mirror Image		
Limited space	Count the Seconds		
Limited space	At the Sports Centre I . . .		
Limited space	Mix 'n' Match		
Limited space	Last Letter First		
Limited space	Don't Break the Chain!		
Limited space	Create a Character		
Limited space	Squeeze Me		
Control, coordination and accuracy	Pass and Repeat		
Control, coordination and accuracy	Don't Let it Fall!		
Control, coordination and accuracy	Olympic Games		
Control, coordination and accuracy	Catch and Release		
Control, coordination and accuracy	Mini Olympics		

Activity checklist

Theme	Activity	When used	Comments										
Control, coordination and accuracy	Quick Release												
Control, coordination and accuracy	Agility Ball												
Control, coordination and accuracy	Bucket Bonanza												
Control, coordination and accuracy	Catchers and Dodgers												
Control, coordination and accuracy	Send and Receive												
Teamwork and cooperation	Hoops 'R' Us												
Teamwork and cooperation	Crocodiles and Alligators												
Teamwork and cooperation	Hot Potato												
Teamwork and cooperation	Find the Set												
Teamwork and cooperation	Keep the Order												
Teamwork and cooperation	Beat the Ball												
Teamwork and cooperation	Steal the Treasure												
Teamwork and cooperation	Number Challenge												
Teamwork and cooperation	Tops 'n' Tails												
Teamwork and cooperation	Vegetable Soup												

Activity checklist

Theme	Activity	When used	Comments
Stamina, speed and agility	Shuttle Relays		
Stamina, speed and agility	Roller Ball		
Stamina, speed and agility	On the Road		
Stamina, speed and agility	Stuck in the Mud		
Stamina, speed and agility	Keep it Moving		
Stamina, speed and agility	Cone Ball		
Stamina, speed and agility	Breathe Hard, Breathe Easy		
Stamina, speed and agility	Feel the Beat		
Stamina, speed and agility	Make a Chain		
Stamina, speed and agility	Through the Legs		
Action rhymes	Them Bones		
Action rhymes	A Sailor went to Sea		
Action rhymes	Hokey Cokey		
Action rhymes	I am a Music Man		
Action rhymes	If You're Happy and You Know It		

Active Every Day: Lower Key Stage 2 © Linda Kelly and Wendy Seward 2006, A & C Black Publishers Ltd

Activity checklist

Theme	Activity	When used	Comments
Action rhymes	Jack and Jill		
Action rhymes	January to December		
Action rhymes	Old Macdonald		
Action rhymes	Ten in the Bed		
Action rhymes	Tennis, Football, Ski and Skate!		
Skipping	Teddy Bear, Teddy Bear		
Skipping	Skipping Challenges		
Skipping	Spanish Dancer		
Skipping	Cross-overs		
Skipping	All in Together, Guys!		
Skipping	Jumping Jacks		
Skipping	Two Little Dickie Birds		
Skipping	Scissor Jumps		
Skipping	Going to a Party		
Skipping	Skip Together		

Bibliography

DfES and DCMS (2003), *PE, School Sport and Club Links Strategy (PESSCL)*

DoH (Spring 2004), *Choosing Health? Choosing Activity: a consultation on how to increase physical activity*

Scheuer, L. J. and Mitchell, D. (2003), *Does Physical Activity Influence Academic Performance?*, SportaPolis newsletter May 2003 (http://www.sports-media.org/sportapolisnewsletter19.htm)

Scottish Executive (2004), *Report of the Review Group on Physical Education*

Index